i

Make Your

OC

The Best

They Can Be!

Katherine LE White

How to Make Your OC the Best They Can Be!

For more information, address: katherinelewhite@katherinelewhite.com

First paperback edition March 2022

Book cover by Carrie Humphrey

Interior art Drey Vogt

ISBN 978-1-95627401-1 (paperback)

www.katherinelewhite.com

Contents

Preface

Let's get the psychological stuff out of the way.

This book is here to help you. It is in no way intended to hurt, belittle, or make you feel less. Especially about your original/personal character. In fact, I am ecstatic that you have made one or lots! I am happy that you have put so much energy into the creative endeavor of creating an entire other being in your mind. And I love that you want to share this person with others in the form of roleplay, story, art, and self-insertion. But there is something we have to talk about before we can move on. And that is:

Criticism

I know that someone criticizing your baby may seem like you are being attacked, but you aren't. Criticism is here to help you. In a way, this is a book of criticism. It tells you what you may be doing wrong with your OC that is turning others off from wanting to interact with them, whether that is them reading a story or role-playing with them.

Of course, that doesn't mean that a person is good at giving criticism or is giving good criticism at all. The definition of criticism is "the analysis of the merits and faults of a work."

Notice it says both merits and faults. When someone is criticizing your OC, or anything really, there is the analysis of the good things and the bad things. And there are *always* good things. Nothing under the sun is all bad. No matter how much we would like to believe so.

Bad criticism is not criticism that you don't like. That is simply criticism that you don't want to hear. Bad criticism is criticism that is pointing out the faults in your work.

Badly given criticism is criticism that is delivered in a poor or hurtful way. You've experienced this, unfortunately too much, which is why I have to write this section in the first place.

Listen to the bad criticism *and* the badly given criticism, even if it hurts your feelings. I do. (And yes, I cry). Don't dismiss it out of hand. It has the seeds of what might make your creative art better. Then again, it might not. That is, in the end, for you to decide. If several people are criticizing you on the same thing, it might be time to look at that aspect of your character creation.

I have added several blank pages at the end of each part of the book for you to write notes. If something in that section or chapter strikes you, jot it down. It struck you for a reason and may be the very thing that makes your OC that much better.

Don't give criticism in a bad way. You don't want it given to you in a way that hurts your feelings, do you? Then don't deliver it in a way that hurts others. Don't be the person who gives criticism in a poorly delivered way. That person is a jerk. Don't be a jerk.

There is a formula that you can use that will help you to keep your fault finding less hurtful for those who have fragile egos but still want to improve their character creation abilities.

merit + fault + merit = criticism sandwich

This is a way that you can couch a bad criticism so that it might be heard by the person you are trying to help. (If you are not trying to help them, then you shouldn't be giving them criticism to begin with). As I said before, even with the most poorly made character, you can find two things that are good about it. Even if it is simply the fact that you are so glad that they made a character and came to you to ask for help.

And in end, it is always your choice whether to take or dismiss the criticism sent your way. It is your character and you can do with it what you will.

Happy creating!

Katherine LE White
character creatrix extraordinaire

Other People Don't Care About Your OC

This is an ugly truth that many a creator of a character does not want to face. But it is true. It is true for you. It is true for me. It is true for everyone who has ever created a character.

No one cares about your OC.

Nor do they have to. No one is under any obligation to care about you or the person you have created. It is an unfortunate reality of free will. However, you are not under any obligation to like anyone else's OC either! So it does go both ways.

Let me give you an example.

Meet Nzinga. She's a vicuna anthro.

Do you care about her? Do you even know what a vicuna is? Or an anthro for that matter? If you do know what a vicuna anthro is, you still probably don't give a rip about her. And why should you? You know nothing about her, other than her race.

Even if we give you a picture of her, without some work on my part, you still don't care about her.

How about now? Do you care about her?
What do you know about her? I guess you
know she's a her and now you might have
an idea what a vicuna is. But why should
you care about her? She's some random
drawing smiling at you from the page. She's
done nothing. She's means nothing. So of
course you don't care.

It is my job to convince you to care about
her.

It is your job to convince people to care
about your OC.

This is what you have to do whether you
are writing a story, engaging in roleplay, or
creating visual artwork. Each of these art

mediums has its own craft that you have to engage in to improve, but they all have the common theme of the artist doing the work to make the onlooker care. The outsider has no obligation whatsoever to give a flying flip about your person, place, or thing.

Make them care!

You have no idea how many people have come to me asking for help with their work and the first thing that we have to deal with is their sense of entitlement. They feel that people must like their character because they have put effort into it. The simple fact that you have put effort into something means nothing to anyone else. It simply means you have put effort into it.

Now, this is a good thing, because if you didn't you wouldn't have a character. And I want you to have a character. I want you to have as many characters as you want to have. But that doesn't mean anyone has to care about them.

So put that entitlement aside. Come to terms with the fact that no one cares about your OC but you. And come to terms with the fact that that is alright. That is the natural order of things. In the same way that lions eat zebras. It isn't good or bad. It simply is.

By now, I know you are saying, "It's been two pages, OC Lady, and you haven't said anything on how to make people care about my OC!" Fear not, my darling character creator. For there are ways to convince the masses to care.

"How?" you ask.

You must suck them into the character. You must make the character so enticing that they cannot help but be drawn in by them. Like being hypnotized by a king cobra, they cannot look away and will wait with bated breath for your next posting on your social media platform of choice.

And how do you do that? By becoming a student of human character. Start watching people. Watch them everywhere, because they are everywhere.

Watch people at school, at work, on the train, on the bus, at the grocery store. Watch them interact with people. Look at their faces and bodies when they speak with people. What do your classmates actually do when they are being yelled at by the teacher? What do their faces look like? Their shoulders? Their hands? What do you think those looks indicate are going through their minds?

What is going through the mind of the people in the grocery store who are looking at the vegetables? How do the people's faces who choose them slowly look as opposed to the faces of the quick choosers? Are there any similarities? Any differences?

These are the kinds of questions I want you to ask yourself about other people as you watch them. As you ask yourself and find your answers, you will gain a greater understanding of people in general. In doing so, you will be able to create imaginary people more realistically.

Another way to learn about people is to learn more about psychology, sociology, and anthropology. Streaming services have shows galore that can tell you all kinds of things about people. Pick something that interests you, and pay attention to how the people think and react about that thing.

You can also work at mastering your craft. Notice I didn't say being a master. I said working at becoming a master of it. The better you are at your craft, the better you are at portraying what is in your mind to the person looking at it.

Are you a drawer? Practice your drawing. Pick one thing and work on it. Decide you are going to get better at arms. Practice them at all angles, the arm muscle defin-ition, the tension and position depending on the emotion of the arms' owner.

Are you a painter? Practice your painting. Pick one thing and work on it. Decide you are going to work on shading. Practice the casing of shadows from light shining at all places, up, down, from the sides. Work on light displaying emotion, soft, sweet, ten-der, hard, harsh, ugly, demonic.

Are you a writer? Practice your writing. Pick one thing and work on it. Practice displaying emotion through the character's action instead of stating it outright, show-ing instead of telling, how the character moves, speaks, comes across on the page.

You don't have the excuse that you don't know how to do any of these things. You have access to the world wide web, where you can learn how to do anything (Unfortu-nately, absolutely anything). You have ac-cess to online communities to people who will help you. How do I know this? Because I'm a member of several. You just have to search them out.

Let's try the example again. I am a writer, so first, we will do it with writing.

Let's meet Nzinga.

Dr. Nzinga Ana looked uncomfortably at the anole-cat hybrid strapped to the table. Her long ears were back and her small mouth was turned downward on her muzzle. The hybrid was straining against his bonds as Dr. Arlid cut a small sample of his skin from a spot that sported no fur. *This is a criminal,* the vicuna reminded herself as she turned her gaze to the clipboard. *And at least this way they are contributing to society.* Her hooves almost slid on the sterile floor, long, soft ears bolting straight upward as the patient on the table began to scream.

Now, do you care about Nzinga a little more? She has a personality. She has cares. She has morals. She has a conflict. All of these things add to you wanting to know more about her.

You can do this with a picture, too. The phrase *A picture is worth a thousand words* is more true than you may realize.

When you look at this drawing the first thing you notice is that Nzinga isn't a human being and that she isn't happy. Her facial features clearly show that she is in distress of some kind. Her brows are creased, her mouth is downturned, her nose is crunched, her ears are back.

Not only that, but the picture isn't a glamor shot of a character. It tells a story. We can tell a huge amount about not only this character, who might not even have a name, but about the world in which she lives. It has doctors. It has labs. It has a high level of science to be able to do sciency things to people on tables. It has lizard-cat things. It has vicuna-people. These people have feelings. They have ideas of right and wrong. And what is happening at the moment might be wrong.

Do you see the difference between the first example and the second?

There are many more details in the second example. You aren't told anything outright. The narrator doesn't tell you what to think, you get to draw your own conclusions. In doing so, I've drawn you in. By tricking you into putting in the mental work, I've increased my chances of getting you to care, of wanting to know what happens to this character.

That is what you have to do.

notes

notes

notes

notes

notes

Your OC Cannot Be All Powerful

We are going to discuss some hard things in this chapter, so you might want to get your hot beverage of choice ready. Mine is a piping hot Irish Breakfast tea with one sugar and milk. It gives me great comfort. Pick the hot beverage that gives you great comfort, for this is the last chapter of "OCs for Beginners" before we get to "Advanced OCs, BYOB".

You've met this character. You've met them more than once. They have won every award in their Academy, graduated valedictorian, was approached by the CIA, FBI, InterPol, StellaPol, AlienPol, and the AOT (Agents of Time). They poo-pooed all of them to become a living god by devising a serum that let them travel through the multiverse, all before the age of 12. Every person they meet falls in love with them, no villain can defeat them, and they stand on a mountain with their hands on their hips as the wind of chance kisses their beautiful face and blows their gorgeous hair behind them.

The dreaded Mary Sue/Gary Stu.

Who exactly is this awful person that we never hope to meet? The term Mary Sue comes from the story "A Trekkie's Tale" in a Star Trek fanzine called Menagerie published in 1973[1] . It was a parody of perfect self-insertion characters, the fantasies that we all want to live out in our favorite fandoms. Mary Sue was half Vulcan, had Cap-

---

1. https://smithsonianmag.com/arts-cult ure/these-women-coined-term-mary-s ue-180972182/ accessed in 2021

tain Kirk fall in love with her instantly, Spock admired her greatly for her logic, she had received the Nobel Peace Prize, the Vulcan Order of Gallantry, and the Tralfamadorian Order of Good Guyhood before dying at the end of the story. All of this at the age of 15.[2] Gary Stu is the male equivalent because it rhymes. I see you now rolling your eyes at the silliness of it all.

We don't want other people to roll their eyes at your character.

A Mary Sue or Gary Stu can be used as a hurtful barb, but if it is ever thrown your way, you might want to take a good look at your OC and see why the person throwing the insult was able to pick up that arrow in the first place.

They are a character that is not only not believable, but they are also too powerful to even suspend belief to let it slide. We talked about several of them when we mentioned those characters described in the last chapter as not being believable.

---

2. https://www.vox.com//2015/12/28/10
   672628/star-wars-force-awakens-rey
   -mary-sue accessed in 2021

They aren't fun to read about or roleplay with.

"Why?" you ask. Because the characters around them have no chance. Of anything. They are a one upper of the utmost degree. The other characters in the story can't get any development because the Mary Sue will steal the page. The other characters in the painting will not get any screen time because the Gary Stu will steal the spotlight. The other characters in roleplay session will not be able to have fun, because the Sue and Stu siblings will not allow them to do anything. They will always be better looking, be more intelligent, have more accolades, be more athletic, and do it with flair and panache.

"How do I keep this awful thing from happening?!" I hear you exclaim. Fear not, for I, too, have exclaimed the exact same thing. It goes back to making your character believable.

Can your OC be defeated in combat? No? They're too powerful.

Can your OC get any person they desire to fall in love with them? Yes? They're too powerful.

Can your OC figure out any puzzle put in front of them? Yes? They're too powerful.

Is there anything that your OC can't do? No? Then your OC is too powerful.

We all want our OCs to have powerful abilities. What's the fun of creating an OC that can't do anything? It isn't that you are creating an OC that can't do anything, but you are creating your OC at a beginning point, not an endpoint. Your OC is going through their origin story. Maybe not the very beginning of their origin story, but even in the middle of it, they aren't the bomb yet.

To keep from making the too powerful OC mistake, I suggest the following formula:

Σ abilities $< \Sigma$ flaws = OC

The sum of your OC's abilities must be less than the sum of your OC's flaws. Or to put it a different way: the sum of your OCs flaws must be greater than the sum of your OC's abilities. They have to have more things wrong with them than right with them in order to equal them out.

I'll give you an example from my own works, so I can't be sued by someone later on for using theirs. If I sue myself, at least I get the money. In my world, Cago, the society is separated into castes divided by animal species. There is a slum section where the hybrids live.

The main female lead in one of the stories, Elke, is a hybrid. By the time we meet her, she is pretty powerful. She's middle-aged. She's one of the top members of the hybrid gang that 'owns' the area. She's a highly visible and successful civil rights activist. She has access to money. With her reindeer blood, she has a strong lower body with a deadly kick. She also has antlers she can use as a weapon should she need to. With her red wolf, she has sharp canine teeth that can rend flesh. With her reptilian blood, she has a resistance to poison. She sounds like she's approaching Mary Sue status. But--

She lives in a world where she has very little civil rights. She is looked down upon by most of society. Just because she has access to money doesn't mean she can use it. The best she can do is a middle-class apartment, not because she can't afford it, but because of her mixed blood, she can't get into a wealthier building. She's not pretty in her society. She is a mishmash of features that come through in her phenotype, neither one thing nor another. She is an unwed mother, not a good thing in her society either. Not only that, it re-inforces a stereotype of hybrids. Her gang territory is small and tight-knit and in the slum. While it's family, it isn't anything to brag about. There are much bigger and better gangs in the city. She has to be on the lookout for getting arrested, as she's not on the good side of the government with her civic activities of equal rights for her people. Her hybrid blood comes with drawbacks. Her avian blood has given her light bones, and she's not getting aches and pains that someone her age might get 20 years later. She has neck problems because her 'bird neck' isn't meant to hold up her deer head with antlers. She's prone to broken bones. Emotionally, she has a major inferiority complex. She knows she's ugly. She gets stared at all the time. She felt the only way to get a family was to be someone's side piece, so she holds the guilt of what the future holds for her two illegitimate children. She has big shoes to fill in the civil rights activist department, as her grandfather started the movement and is still alive. Her brother is a lawyer and she's 'only' a therapist. She lost both of her parents at a young age and was raised by her grandparents, so making them proud is very important to her. She is deathly afraid to fail. And she is utterly aware that she is muddied in a society that values purity.

(If you want to find out more about Elke, go check out Entangled Oaths on Kindle Vella.)

Do you see how much longer the flaws paragraph is than the abilities? That's on purpose. You do that so that you don't end up with a Mary Sue or Gary Stu. Did I mention that's not fun? It's not fun to read. It's not fun to see. It's not fun to roleplay with. So let's not do it.

notes

notes

notes

notes

notes

Your OC Must Be Believable

You have your OC all made, have a background made up, a personality developed, likes and dislikes, all the stuff you are supposed to have for your OC. You've worked on your craft, you've made an effort and…..still, no one will interact with you.

What did you do wrong?

Is your character believable?

The people you are interacting with, whether they are viewers, readers, or players, have to be able to identify with your character in some way. If they can't, they are not going to be interested (read: not care about your OC).

We interact with things we have to interact with or want to interact with. Others don't have to interact with your OC. So they have to want to. Sometimes, wanting them to takes work.

If your character doesn't resonate with people on a personal level, they will gloss over your OC and move on to one that is more relatable.

I was literate roleplaying with a character once, and the fellow did nothing but sigh depressedly. He did nothing. He just acted dejected and sighed and looked this way and that and was totally no fun to interact with. I tried to draw this person out. I am a good literate roleplayer. I can usually come up with something to move the narrative forward. This person was not having it. He was just sighing despondently. It got the point that I had to say, "Dude, you have to give me something to go on here!"

The guy answered me with, "I do this all the time and no one else has problems roleplaying with me."

I seriously doubt that, because this individual was always asking for free players for his one character, whereas others are beating invitations off with a stick. Why? Because someone doing nothing but being a depressed sigher isn't believable. And if they are, no one wants to be around that person, so why would they want to engage in an escapist activity with them?

How do you make them more believable? Let's go through a run-of-the-mill character sheet and find out.

Character sheets usually consist of a name, class of some type, age, gender, species, sexuality, appearance, likes, dislikes, and (perhaps) an array of numbers that will indicate what kind of character traits your character has that make up a personality and a biography. All the ins and outs that make up a person on a piece of paper. We will go through each one individually to see how you can refine yours to make your OC the best they can be.

Name: What's in a name? That which we call a rose would still smell as sweet. Add endnote I hate to disagree with good old Billy, but there most definitely is something in a name. When thinking of a name, you have to take into account what you want to get out of the name. Are you looking for a cultural identity? Ease of pronunciation? Commonality?

Don't name your character Chad or Karen, and then get upset when no one knows which dude or dudette your character is because everyone is named Chad or Karen. Or Malik and Beyonce.

On the opposite hand, don't name your characters Arathusius and Shanintandia and get upset when people can't pronounce them. People are lazy and don't want to sound them out. Accept the fact that people don't want to.

It doesn't mean that you *can't* name your characters those names. Just don't get upset when you come up with hiccups around those names.

A good way to get around this problem, no matter what the name is, common or not, is to make the name mean something. I have a dormouse character in my world named Terpsichore. Dormice are the smallest of mice. She is a nurse. And because she was so small, her parents decided to give her a big name. But guess what. Everyone I talk to her about calls her Terp.

Do you have an orc character? Their language is supposed to be very brutish, no? Let's say we name this dude Gl'rgruk. We have named him this it is guttural, with the r being swallowed (as shown by the '). We will say that it means, gl'r=sun and gruk=ash. So he is The Sun turns to Ash. Which means, in orcish, he is going to turn your body in a flaming pile of gray stuff in the middle of the day. Beware. His parents gave him this name because he was tiny when he was born. They prayed every day that he would grow into his name. Luckily, he is now average sized. Not quite Sun-Ash, but he isn't Teeny-Tiny-Make-Fun-Of-You-Warrior-Orc either, so his parents are satisfied. He might have a bit of an inferiority complex.

Or, you can be simple. Her parents named her Jane. They named her Jane because her grandmother was named Jane. That's it. What relationship Jane had with Jane is up to you as you create both Janes.

Age: This is how old your character is. This should be pretty straightforward, but for some people, it isn't. This is one designation where people want to make their character 'special' or 'different' and end up making their character into a cliché or a hack.

Be reasonable when you think about your age. Is your character on a starship and 14 years old? Then no, they are not the Captain. They aren't the Captain at 18 either. Or 28. At 38, maybe. Look up how old ship captains are. They usually get promoted at 43-45 years of age, and get in charge of a ship at 49-51. Your 38 year old is young to be in charge of her Starship of the Royal Navy of the Great Empire of Oooga Booga.

If we use the example of literate roleplay, when someone encounters your character and sees that your 16 year old high schooler is a skilled assassin with 32 kills on their record, the other player is going to make assumptions about you. (I know we aren't supposed to make assumptions, but we do. It's human nature.) The assumption they are going to make is that you don't know how to roleplay well because you don't know how to build a believable character. So they won't play with you.

Why? Because high schoolers are not assassins. I dare you to find me a 16 year old assassin. Or an assassin that is in high school. Assassins are adults for a reason because it takes years and years and years to become proficient enough to be able to sneak into places and silently kill people. 16 year olds haven't lived long enough to learn that. Not only that, if they are learning how to be assassins, they are not in high school where you are able to roleplay with them. They are out in some weird assassin complex learning to be assassins. Again, where you cannot roleplay with them.

Don't have your 16 year old high school student be an assassin at night when no one is watching. Assassins are psychopaths (yes, they are, they have to be to do their jobs) and high skilled and not in high school.

In other words, be reasonable. You can make your character special. You can make them different. But don't do it in a way that makes other players roll their eyes. If it seems ridiculous, then it probably is. Give some thought to your character's age in relation to where they are and what they know. Don't be a cliché or a hack.

Class: This category means different things in different places, but most often goes with a character's chosen occupation. When delving into this section of your character's development, keep in mind what a person in your character's profession would and wouldn't know or how they would or wouldn't think. These will have a great bearing on how they act or what job they have.

I used to teach kindergarten to at-risk children. They were at-risk for lots of things. Being lethargic was not one of them. In case you haven't noticed from my writing style, I'm not at risk for being lethargic either. That was good, otherwise, we would have been a very poor match. A person with lower energy would have died at my job. They'd have lasted a week and then not have had enough energy to drive their car to come in the following Monday. Conversely, if I had an office job, my coworkers would hate me. I would make so much noise pacing up and down the aisle, tapping my pen, humming or singing, clicking my heels, talking to people, getting up and stretching...they would conspire to make me have an unfortunate accident so that I would be unable to return to work for a long time. That is if I didn't get fired first.

Your elven ranger isn't going to a clumsy oaf so bad that they continuously fall out of trees and break limbs. She would have been kicked out of ranger school. Or already killed by falling out of a tree. Your otter anthro isn't going to be unable to swim, it is in his DNA. Now, that doesn't mean they can't be a little of those things. Your elven ranger can have bad aim, but bad doesn't mean abominable. Your otter can be the not-greatest of swimmers, but he can still swim. Put your characters at a disadvantage. Don't make them absurd. That just makes it look like you don't know what you're doing.

Species: What race of being are you? A dingbat? A ghost? A vorhou from the planet Omnicron? Species itself is a rare place where a player will get hitched up, it is in the specs of the species that glitch them.

So you want to be a vorhou from the planet Omnicron. You want your vorhou to be 6 feet tall. But vorhous don't come 6 feet tall. The tallest they get is 4 feet 10 inches. "No matter!" you announce. "I shall make my vorhou half-human, so that they can become 6 feet tall. They now just look like a 6 feet tall vorhou."

It looks like you've solved the problem. But let's dig a little deeper.

Firstly, can vorhous and humans have kids? And if they do, what's the likelihood that the kid is going to look exactly like a fullblood vorhou except for their height? Their different species, not different phenotypes (they look different) of the same species. They are way too tall to be vorhou, so they are mixed with something. This will cause problems in their world. You have now, essentially, given them a form of giantism. Do you want to play a character with a form of giantism where nothing fits or is built to their frame?

Secondly, is it ok for vorhous to have interracial kids? Will they be discriminated against on Omnicrom? Are you willing to play a character that is a target of systematic discrimination? "I'll just have them be on Earth." Ok. They have the same problem in the vorhou community on Earth. And if they live with humans, they are the odd one out, they don't look human at all and don't grow up to be a vorhou in anything but looks.

Thirdly, which should have been firstly, are there even vorhous in the universe in which you are playing? Because you can want to be a vorhou, or a dragon, or a honeybee, or a human being, but if you are playing my world of Cago, they don't exist, so you are out of luck. I mean, you can't be a person that can't manifest in a certain imaginary space, as paradoxical as that might sound.

Do you see where I am going with this? Just because you think it might be super cool to have a really big vorhou (and it may be super cool to have a really big vorhou), that doesn't make it believable. Or, more accurately, it doesn't make the way you want to play it believable.

Be sure to consider that when creating their DNA make up.

Gender/Sexuality: I've lumped these together because it is difficult to separate them at this moment in history. I am going to start with defining terms, I find that many people do not even know what gender and sexuality really are. I got my degree is anthropology, so knowing the real definition of these anthropological, scientific concepts is important to me and to society as a whole.

Gender is the role one plays in society. Society is made up of individuals who all play parts in it, like in a play. Those parts are split into three categories, masculine, feminine, and neutral (notice I did not say male or female). Any male or any female can fill any role.[1] Perhaps not without ridicule, but anyone can fill that role in the play that is society (free-Western society, anyway). So Richard can be a stay-at-home dad and knitting sweaters and socks for the kids while Bertha can be a construction worker and bring home the bacon for Richard and the brood. These roles are culturally constructed, so what is appropriate in one society at one time may not be appropriate in another. For example, knitting used to be only a manly way back when, used by fishermen to make nets.[2] Now we think of it as an old grandma sport. Pants used to only be worn by Persian women, everyone else in the known world wore some form of

---

1. https://gender.jhpiego.org/analysistoo lkit/gender-concepts-and-definitions accessed in 2021

2. https://sustainable-fashion-collective.c om/2017/05/04/brief-knitting-history -uses accessed in 2021

a skirt.[3] Gender roles can, do, and should change over time.

Sex, as a noun, is the stuff in one's pants. The genitalia that a person has is one's sex. It is in this context we use the words male and female.

Sexual intercourse, which we often shorten to "sex" is a verb and is one of the things you can choose to do with your sexuality.

Sexuality is the conglomeration of thoughts, feelings, behaviors, and attractions that a person has toward others (notice I said nothing about sex or sexual intercourse). Attractions include emotional attractions and physical attractions. Sexuality, in reality, is a very complex thing, because it includes both emotional and physical attractions. Where the line of friend and potential lover is in one's mind can be very blurry at a certain point. Sexuality comes in three variants (with lots of tiny little subvariants) across a continuum. Those are homosexuality, which means a person is attracted to the same sex; bisexuality,

---

3. https://kingandallen.co.uk/journal/201
6/a-brief-history-of-trousers accessed
in 2021

which means one is attracted to both sexes; and heterosexuality, which means one is attracted to the opposite sex.

A person can fall anywhere on that line.

A fourth designation, asexuality, means one is not on the continuum at all. this is *very* simplified and we could go into a whole scientific bruhaha here (and oh, do I want to), but we won't, because that isn't what this book is about. We will, however, continue our discussion about creating your character now that we have defined our terms.

Appearance: What does your character look like? That's an easy question to answer, right? She's wearing this or that. He has piercings here or there. Their hair is this color or that color or lots of colors.

I am constantly surprised by how many people have trouble with this. They have no clear idea of what their person looks like in their head. You are creating a person. At the very least, know what they look like!

When you get to this part of the process, and for most people, this is actually the first part of the process, be as detailed as you can.

Be specific with hair/fur color, and not just /insert color of your choice here/ . Is it light, dark, medium? Do an internet search on hair colors, or just colors in general if your character has a non-conventional hair color. My natural hair color is titian. Do you even know what that is? Look it up. Now you do. Hair isn't just brown, blond, black, red. There are shades. Find out what they are and used them.

What is their face shape? Of course include the classic oval/circle/square/triangle. But go deeper. Is their face open or closed? Long or short? Do you know what that means? Research! I have two deer skulls in my gaming room, and you can see the difference in the face structure of the two fellows. One's eye sockets are larger and closer together and the other's are smaller and farther apart. To the human eye, one of those skulls, the larger, closer together eyed one, was probably a prettier buck. These details make a difference in your overall character design and how you play them and others see them.

Do this same process with their entire body-torso, arms, legs, hands, feet, fingers, toes, shoulders, hips. All of these details make your character more clear to you, both physically and psychologically. How we perceive we look plays a huge role in how we feel about ourselves. So knowing exactly how your OC looks can give you huge insights into their character.

It also gives an illustrator, if you are not a visual artist (ahem, me), lots of references for drawing or painting your character for you when you commission one!

Likes and Dislikes: This one is a personal pet peeve of mine. For more than one reason.

Firstly, I learn my characters as I play them, so I don't always know what they like and dislike. But it is something you have to put down on the paper or screen before you start interacting with other people. (Luckily with story writing, you don't. You can fill in as you go).

Secondly, people commonly fill these in with only three items such as, "ice cream, cats, and moonlight." Come on, you can't come up more than that. Everyone likes ice cream, cats, and moonlight. Only weird people don't like ice cream, cats, and moonlight. Ok, maybe normal people don't like cats, but still.

This category isn't just meant to be for surface things. Those things can get you to know a character, but *why* don't they like those things? Why do they like ice cream? Or not like ice cream? Do they dislike ice cream because it is cold? Because is too sweet? Because it hurts their teeth? Because it smells like curdled milk? Because it brings back a bad memory? All of these things can be indicated by "dislikes: ice cream" but none of them really tell us what the character dislikes. They *actually* dislike cold. Or pain. Or sweets. Or acrid smells. Or whatever feeling the bad memory evokes. It isn't the ice cream at all, but what the ice cream represents.

Dig deep. What does your character really like? I mean, put "ice cream, cats, and moonlight." But list other things also. What do they desire? That's a like. Do they like feeling like they belong? Do they dislike people who talk too much? Do they like warm places and dislike the cold? Do they dislike being told what to do? Or perhaps they like being told what to do because it gives them a sense of belonging and caring and control in their lives.

Makes these some deep down good stuff. Not "spiders, things with six legs, and little brothers."

Personality: An excellent way to begin to describe your character is to decide if they are an introvert or an extrovert. Again, we are going to define terms, because these two words are very often misconstrued for things they do not represent. Misrepresentation is bad, whether it is with words or people.

Introverts get their personal energy tank filled by being alone. It doesn't mean that they don't like people. Many an introvert has discovered they liked people way more than they thought when lockdown occurred for a year. A person who doesn't like people is a misanthrope. If we want to be nice, we can say a cynic. (Though misan-thropes and cynics tend to be introverts). Introverts are people who need their alone time in order to function to their full capac-ity. This is why they tend to choose qui-et occupations or hobbies. Subconsciously, they realize they need that alone time in order to be there for the people in their lives they do spend time with. They tend to be task oriented and time conscious.

Extroverts get their personal energy tank filled by being with people. It doesn't mean they are constant party goers, non-stop talkers, and emotional vampires (though these people do tend to be extroverts). It means that if they spend too much time by themselves, they get caught up in their own heads, drowning in their own stuff, and see no way out. They need other peo-ple in their lives in a way that introverts do not. Having others around energizes them. They usually don't care what the task is, as long as they are spending it with the peo-ple they want to be spending it with. Their sense of time is usually not the greatest, again because they are people-centric, not time oriented.

These two traits are on a continuum, with the extremes of a misanthrope and emotional vampire at the two ends. Most of us fall somewhere in the middle.

Introvert		Extrovert
misanthrope	Equally introverted and extroverted	Emotional vampire

With just these two definitions to go on, you can create a character personality that is detailed enough for any play, visual art, or story. I am sure you know you know by now what I am going to suggest about where to put your precious creation on the continuum of vert-dom. Unless you are creating a supervillain , which I suggest you do not, stay away from the extremes. They are exceedingly rare, despite what we say about someone hating people or sucking others dry. Those people are psychopaths, sociopaths, or narcissists, which only make up 3.7% of the general population. [4] 3.7

---

4. https://www.psychologytoday.com/us/blog/5-types-people-who-can-ruin-your-life/201804/are-narcissists-and-sociopaths-increasing

% of anything isn't believable. That's why people who deal with real life sociopaths, psychopaths, and narcissists are not believed. (It's called Cassandra syndrome, by the way.)

Put your character somewhere between the two extremes and then play them on that point on the continuum.

Biography: This is the one that is hardest and usually makes players have to go back and tweak their characters. When writing your character's biography, remember, there is a reason for everything. Nothing happens in a vacuum. Your precious baby did not fall from the aether. You need to know the life story of your character. Oh, you don't need to know every little detail, but you do need to know a fair amount about your character's personal history. You do not need to know names, per se, but you do need to know broad strokes, so that the lens that informs how your character sees the world is a little more in focus.

What kind of household did your character grow up in? A two parent or single parent? Both parents' working? What kind of occupations did their parents have or not have? Were they poor, working class, middle class, or wealthy? Did they have lots of friends? A few friends? No friends? Are they the oldest, middle, or youngest child in their family?

That is basic family information you should know about your character. All of these will have an impact on your character's personality and decisions. Or the other way around, perhaps you have chosen to portray your character a certain way, and giving them one of these personal historical lenses explains why they act they do.

Does your character have PTSD? Why? And do you know how to play out PTSD? Do you want to play out PTSD? Does the why even make sense? Things don't just drop out of the sky and cause problems. There is a cause and effect, and every effect has a cause. Does your character have amnesia? Why? Do you know how to play out a character with amnesia? Have you done your research? The bigger the 'thing', the more research and detailed the reason needs to be. You have to convince the other players, readers, and viewers that you know what you're talking about and this reason is a valid reason, that this life you're trying to sell us is a valid life.

Now remember, your character doesn't have to be used and abused, either. That trope is way overplayed, by the way. They can be just normal, everyday people. They can be everyday jerks, because they were raised in a bigoted home that feels all vorhous should be segregated because your character's dad was assaulted one day. They can be a sweet, innocent person that loves everyone and can't understand why they can't make friends with all the cute little vorhous, because their parents wanted to raise a kid that didn't see species and were actually successful. What is important is that their life story makes sense. Always ask why, and if you can't come up with a why, then that detail probably doesn't need to be included in their lives.

I know this is a lot to absorb, and don't expect yourself to absorb it all in one go. Your character is always a work in progress, and so is your understanding of people. The more you work on making your character believable, the more enjoyable the entire experience of working with your character will be.

notes

notes

notes

notes

notes

Your OC Must Have A Life

I feel that this should be self-evident, but for some reason, it is not. Many people want their OC to be such a shining star that they forget, either purposefully or not, they need to do ordinary things too. Even the greatest of superheroes (and supervillains) needs to take a dump. And when they do, they do it on a toilet, just like you and me. At least, I hope you are pooping on a toilet.

Your OC does stuff *other* than the cool stuff that we tend to see on screen. Your hero is not always saving the world. Your villain is not always scheming their next heist. Your OC is doing ordinary stuff too.

Some of that ordinary stuff is important. And it can be interesting! I want to see that beefcake OC of yours that you are always drawing in weightlifter poses being at the bar and shot down by someone pretty. I want to see your scientist who is always making incredible inventions mess up and end up with their hair on fire while someone else tries to put it out with a can of cola. I want to see that guy cuddling on the couch with his wife watching TV and their kid nestled between them, like a candid photo.

For your OC to have depth, they need to have a life. They need stuff to do other than the fun and fancy stuff that they do. They need slice of life stuff that they do. Do they garden? Do they knit? Do they raise eaglets? Do they ride a unicycle?

How do they do their laundry? Their grocery shopping? What do they do when they are lonely? What do they watch on TV? What do they read? Do they have a pet? Do they have a pesky landlady? Do they have a nosy neighbor? Is their mom always trying to set them up with someone?

I know many of these questions may seem silly or mundane, but knowing the answer to some of them will make your OC more believable.

This is especially true if your OC is part of an established canon and works within a canonized storyline. They cannot be with the on-screen team all the time. In fact, they shouldn't be an integral part of the on-screen team.

People like the on screen canon team for a reason. Because they are the on-screen canon team. So you can't be upset when you make your OC the seventh member of The Snooters and rewrite all of the adventures with your OC in them and no one likes your stories. Firstly, you've created a self-insertion, which is perfectly fine, but that's for you, not other people. Secondly, you've created a Mary Sue or Gary Stu or something closely related to them.

So your job is to create your OC in an interesting way within the established fandom without fudging things around too much. Remember, it is your job to make the viewer/reader/player care about your OC, not for them to care about your OC simply because you made them. And just because you've plugged them in as the seventh Snooter doesn't make them interesting or care-about-able, despite how much we care about the six Snooters.

"How, OC Lady? How do I do this?" you ask.

You do it in the spaces in the fandom.

Because all of us come from spaces in other people's lives. We literally came from a space in our parents' lives. There was no baby growing in the particular woman's belly that was your birth mother, and then after a (hopefully pleasant) encounter with your birth father, there you were. Our friends come to us through spaces in our lives. You go to school and work, and in between the spaces where you are actually doing what you're supposed to be doing while you're there, you meet people. Some of them you like and some you don't. The ones that you do like you spend more time with (spaces in between the working) until they become your friends.

There is no need to force a space from which your character emerges. When you do this, it makes your character trite from the very beginning. You've lost a huge potential audience before you've even begun, simply because of the awkward and/or un-believable entrance of your OC. In any canon fandom, empty spaces abound.

Take a look at the canon story. It doesn't matter what fandom it is. Take a look at it and find a space in it. It might be a tiny space, like the one in the original Star Wars trilogy. In A New Hope, the line "Many peo-ple died to get this information," spawned an entire movie of its own--Rogue One. That is a space in a story and exploding it.

Your space doesn't have to be that big. It can be the time in between The Snoot-ers going out and coming back home. It can be the three weeks between scenes 5 and 6 in episode 32 of The Snooters. It can be the bartender. It can be the kid of the nosy neighbor. Your OC can still have adventures with The Snooters. With all of them or with one or two of them. But they are side adventures, not the ones that are on-screen for the entire world to see from the TV show, or the book series, or the comic series, or the movies. They are side stories that we don't get to see or read. That makes your OC so much more inter-esting to everyone.

I'll give another example from my own work. In *Entangled Oaths*, there is an entire city of spaces to explore. Cago is out there to walk and run and bike ride. In many of the chapters, the Chief Diversity Officer, Davin, who is in charge of population control is having a meeting with the rest of the C-Suite that rule the city. Davin is all that and a bag of chips. Women want him and men want to be him and some men want him and some women want to be him. Instead of creating a love interest for him (which would be hard to do keeping him in character, he's a player), why not create an OC that is one of his household? One of his servants, perhaps? Oh, Davin isn't all that and a bag of chips, you say? He doesn't do all those things on his own? He needs other people to help him in the background and he gets all the credit? Why, you OC, now you have a life and many adventures to go on in all the beautiful spaces in the story.

Because of these spaces, we can relate to a character that comes from them, because we come from the same place. We aren't famous. We aren't all that and a bag of chips. Neither are the characters that come from the empty spaces in canon.

Now, I fully expect you to go and write all about The Snooters, because I haven't yet, so there is a huge space open for you to run in.

notes

notes

notes

notes

notes

Your OC Must Evolve Over Time

No one starts out fully cooked. This ties in closely with our OCs not being all powerful. Everybody starts out as a nobody and your OC has to make movement toward an emotional/spiritual/psychological destination. In essence, when one consumes a story, that is what they are doing, experiencing the movement of a character from one place to another. It might be a physical place, but more often than not, it isn't physical. It is a movement of the mind, of problems that are thrown in the character's way, and dealt with in one way or another.

Remember those flaws we talked about? Now is when they really come into play. These flaws are the obstacles that your OC is working through. It is part of their movement through time until they "arrive". And arriving doesn't happen when your character is 25 either. Unless they die then. If I had been all finished at 25, I would have lived a sad, sad life. There is still lots of life left in this old clunker--I'm firmly middle-aged at the time of this writing and I still haven't "arrived."

The classic hero's journey is a clear cut example of this evolution, the movement of a character both physical and psychological. The character starts in the ordinary world, and by the end of the adventure, has ascended to a higher realm. That realm is usually the knowledge or wisdom attained that others do not have.

It starts with a call to adventure, the beginning of the story. Something happens to get the sedentary character moving. There are the many obstacles and tests that the character must go through while finding their friends and enemies along the way. They face their deepest, darkest self, their ugly self, the self that is capable of doing awful things and vanquish it (maybe). At this point, the character makes a new decision on how to see the world. Their lens has changed. After this, they grow to become the best them they can be (this is where we get our superheroes and supervillains). They have arrived! Until eventually they return back home, forever changed and filled with the special knowledge that made them who they are.

Notice how there is a lot of movement in that paragraph. Yeah, your OC needs to do that. They need to move along the path. And the path is a spiral, filled with smaller paths that lead to larger and larger paths, much like a whisk. The one I described is just the big one.

If you are dazed from the giant spiral I just sent you on, snap out of it. It isn't as daunting as it seems. You've worked really hard on making your OC believable as far as their background and abilities, right? Right? If not, go back to the beginning and do that. I'll wait.

Now that you've done that, getting your OC to move along emotionally/psychologically seems hard, but it isn't. A good way to get started is to give your OC a conscious want. What do they want? I mean, really want? I'm not talking about chocolate bars or a million dollars. I mean, **really** want?

All people have a deep driving need. The ultimate need we all have is to belong. It drives almost everything we do. People are willing to die in order to belong to a group. But just below that one is another deep-seated need that your OC will have (yes, you have one, too). It is broad, like belonging, and it colors the lens through which we see the world.

Core Values
Your character needs something more than anything else in the world. This something subconsciously informs everything that your character does, even if the character doesn't realize it. It is the internal arc of your character's story, starting from not having this deep need met to realizing what it is and getting it met to their satisfaction.

This deep seated need is called a core value.

Here are a list of core values that your character might have:
- Freedom

- Compassion

- Fairness

- Security

- Truth

- Integrity

- Belonging

Your character won't have all of these core values, only one or two. You can see that it is a broad longing that can be met in a myriad of ways. But the core value that your character has is the lens through which all of their decisions are made.

None of these values are good or bad. The actions that stem from them can be interpreted on a spectrum. One may have the core value of belonging and be very accepting of everyone, because they want them to belong. They could also be very tribal and not accepting of anyone new, because they do not belong or threaten their sense of belonging.

Freedom

Freedom is the absence of control over your character. A person who has freedom as a core value is often a rebel or troublemaker. They don't take orders well and sometimes have a 'you can't make me' attitude. They are often competitive and strive for excellence in what they do, wanting recognition for their accomplishments. They may be a quiet resistance fighter or a loud civil rights leader. It can also involve freedom for a singular purpose, such as creative independence; knowledge gathering, financial gain, fame, or self-respect.

Compassion

Compassion is concern for the suffering or misgivings of others. People with this core value tend to be in the helper professions—doctors, nurses, caregivers, and teachers. They value helping others and society as a whole. They are usually rather affectionate. Their care for others makes them lean toward a very democratic group dynamic so that all members can be involved in decision making.

Fairness

Fairness is the impartial treatment of others. This can go hand in hand with compassion, but doesn't have to. Those who have a core value of compassion and fairness tend to get along very well. Those with this core value care very much about ethical practices and honesty, even if they are not the kindest solution. They take a strong role in democratic group dynamics so that all members can be given consideration in making decisions, even if they are not directly involved.

Security

Security is being free from danger or threat. This is a very primal core value, one that everyone holds at some level. But if a character has this as their driving core value, they will be drawn to order and efficiency. They also tend to be attracted by wealth, power, and authority, as they see these things as ways to stay secure from other people and circumstances. Efficiency, order, and effectiveness do not have to have a compassionate or democratic component to them. To be most secure, someone must make decisions for others that will cause them to be less secure. Therefore, these characters tend to be followers rather than trailblazers. They will take the road most traveled, because it has the known result of being the most secure.

Truth

Truth is that which is in accordance with fact or reality. It is a very integral core value to those who want to operate on a growth mindset. It evolves into ideals such as wisdom, putting the truth into viable action; inner harmony, being at peace with oneself. Oftentime religiosity, the condition of being very religious, stems from this core value. The individual who is religious is convinced of their truthfulness

Integrity

Integrity is the quality of having strong principles. Individuals who have integrity operate from a place of certainty, they are sure of what they are doing most of the time. They tend to be very competent and decisive. They have a sense of responsibility and accountability to themselves and others. Their decisions are made through the lens of the principle(s) that they hold.

Belonging

Belonging is a sense of inclusion in society at some level. It can be on the small level, that of a family. Or a larger level, as a citizen of a country. It involves community of any kind; close relationships; friendships; meaningful work; loyalty of others to the character and the character's loyalty to other people and ideas.

Almost every person has a deep sense of wanting to belong. Some psychologists would argue that this doesn't go on the list, as it is a universal psychological need rather than an individual need. That is for you to decide with your character as you create them. Think long and hard to where your character feels or doesn't feel they belong.

This is a core value that your OC holds. There are many more than the list above, but you get the idea. A core value is not just a belief that your OC holds. A belief can be changed. A core value is one that is stuffed down deep inside of you, and likely never to change in one's entire lifetime. If your OC has this core value, it's there to stay. How they exhibit this core value may change.

That's a want, and that's what we are looking for. This want is usually not at all reasonable, because it was created by the subconscious mind. What makes it different than other subconscious wants is that somehow the conscious mind managed to get ahold of it. If in a logical argument, your OC and my OC would probably admit that it is unreasonable, that it is ultimately completely unattainable. But--they would also argue, it is *partially* attainable. That's where your OC's movement comes in.

Do they want no one to tell them what to do? Do they want to never feel hurt? Do they want to ever go hungry? Do they want everyone to feel the pain they felt? Do they want all slugs wiped from the Earth? Do they want to eliminate the elusive OC Lady?

What is it that drives your OC forward? That unattainable thing can get you started if you can't come up with anything else, until something smaller and more fun comes along.

Your OC must make movement in the story, in the picture, in the play, they must evolve, going from one place to another. Really, they must. No one and nothing in the universe is stagnant. Everything changes, even if those changes are imperceptible to us. But it is those changes that make a reader/viewer/player want to invest in your OC. Do your emotional work by giving your OC their emotional work to do.

notes

notes

notes

notes

notes

You and Your OC: Self-Insertion

T his is a sticky subject, I know. But like criticism, it is one I think should be addressed.

It is also one that I wish was not sticky. I think that self-insertion is a fine thing. In fact, psychologically, it is a very healthy thing.[1] It increases creativity and problem-solving abilities, holds off dementia-type diseases, improves general mental health, can help with more specified mental health conditions, and is generally a lot of fun. You can use your OC to help you deal with your real-life problems, trying out different roles and responsibilities. Self-insertions can teach us empathy by pretending to be someone else, in a different position in life and society, walking a mile in someone else's shoes, so to speak. By pretending to be someone else, we can learn huge lessons about how others see the world around us. This leads to great leaps in compassion which helps both the self-inserter and those around them.

One of the most powerful things that self-insertion does is show us that the roles and feelings that we have in our real lives are of our own making to a large extent. It teaches us that we have much more control over our lives than we think we do. If we can change the way we feel by playing

---

1. https://www.psychologytoday.com/us/blog/moral-landscapes/202012/how-play-adult

pretend as an OC in a story or roleplay, whether it is feeling good or bad, by changing our thoughts in play, we can do it in our real lives, too.

My very first OC was a self-insertion from my childhood and that character is still alive and kicking today. I plug her in each iteration of the fandom in which they originate when I daydream to wind down at night. This OC, Illusionna keeps me from staying up all night thinking about my own universe and stories. I know I can't do anything commercial with her. She lives completely in a universe that belongs to a large corporation. That universe is deep and well developed, so I do no worldbuilding and little story building either. I just plug her in wherever it is I want her to be in the canon, or not canon storyline and let her drift as she will until I drift to sleep.

I get to explore what a being might experience when they have a million-year lifespan. It can't be birthdays. Is it how the stars move in the sky? Is it by the number of new individuals who come into one's life? Is the number of times that body parts are replaced? I can imagine what it is like to be part of a species that has known nothing but war for the majority of its existence.

How does that affect how one thinks? What is the lens through which one sees the world? I can imagine how their society is set up through that lens. How decisions would be made and why those decisions would be made. I can think of what life might be like not being an organic life form. How would that inform my entire worldview?

Self-insertion does come with a warning. WARNING!

You see the big yellow sign that says warning?

Self-insertion is for you. It isn't for anyone else. It is for you. Say it again. Self-insertion is for you.

When we put ourselves into an OC, we are doing just for us. It isn't for the reader, or the viewer, or the player. It is solely for me, myself, and I. This is something that you must keep in mind when dealing with other people and your OC. It harkens back to rule number one, but in bold, italics, and yellow highlighter. In fact, I suggest you highlight it now. **No one cares about your OC.** When it comes to a self-insert, no one cares even more. And that isn't a bad thing, darling. Honest, it isn't. It just is. Like poop is brown. Hopefully your poop is brown. Otherwise go to the doctor.

Self-insertion is a wonderful way for an individual to spread their wings and play pretend long after playing pretend is considered acceptable. I am middle-aged and I still play pretend. Every single day. Several times a day. It fills my life with magic and joy, gives me immense happiness, and harms absolutely no one. So why in the world would I not do it?

However, this harkens back to no one caring about your OC. Or in the case of my pretending, my OC. If I want to share my pretending, in the form of self-insertion, you have to make them care. But you are already well on your way to doing that, now aren't you?

notes

notes

notes

notes

notes

notes

notes

notes

Dear Reader

Dear Reader,

    This book has been a long time in the making. It started out as an article written years ago in the fanfic community and has made the rounds in many different incarnations as I tried to help people improve on their literate roleplay and fanfiction skills. I saw a need for something cohesive and evergreen. Hence, this little booklet. I hope it has helped you.

    If you would like to stay abreast of my latest stories, of which I always have something coming out, please consider subscribing to my newsletter. I'll never spam you. You'll get first dibs on all my work, and discounts on my books when they first come out.

I have a favor to ask of you. Please return to the platform where you bought this book (amazon, Barnes & Nobel, d2d) and leave an honest review. Tell me and others what you thought of the story. Reviews are an author's bread and butter, it is how I get seen in the slew of stories that are out there and all the help I get by you, my loyal readers, is greatly appreciated. And since reviews don't transfer from platform to platform, if you could copy and paste your review onto the reader site of your choice (goodreads, bookbub, etc.) I would also greatly appreciate that.

If you would like to contact me, there are a myriad of ways to do so on most social media outlets and my website <u>Missives from a Hummingbird</u>. I will answer all correspondence I get, I just can't guarantee that it will be answered in a timely manner. Hummingbirds are known for their flightiness, after all.

Yours flightfully,

Katherine LE White

Thank You

No book is written by itself, no matter what the author line says. This book is no different. It has passed through many hands to get to yours and I wish to think those hands.

To my husband Matt, who encouraged me to get this book down on paper. 26 years is a long time to be together.

To Lydia Wiese, for editing it and giving me advice as she always does. Her support and being a fan of *me* has saved my writing career more than once.

To Carrie Humphrey, without whom there would be no cover. To any of my books! You can contact her at HHBSPubl ishing@gmail.com

To Drey Vogt, who did the interior illustrations of Nzinga. If you would like to commission them, contact them at https://weather.crd.co/

And to you, for buying, reading, and taking the advice in this book. May your OC be the best they can be!

About Katherine LE White

Katherine L. E. White is an award-winning poet, essayist, and international best-selling fiction writer, who has had the privilege of growing up all over the world. A rare beauty with green eyes and crazy titian curls, she goes about having grand (mis)adventures with her family and many friends, and then tries hard not to write about them. She often champions the causes of those on the fringes of society in her writing, while pretending to be an urban farmer in real life. Pretending being the operative word. If others were to rely on her skills to eat, they would most assuredly starve. She lives in Southern Appalachia with her husband, two children, and several animals, all of whom, thankfully, are better urban farmers than she is. She is also featured in every department of the Organization of Transformative Works, except the legal advocacy section. She is, after all, not a lawyer. If you'd like to know more about her, visit her website at http://www.katherinelewhite.com/

Also By Katherine LE White

Entangled Oaths

The Therian Initiative
Man of Light and Shadow
Lady of Lost Souls

With Michael Bruce Edwards
Murder at the Panionic Games
Murder at the Festival at Apaturia
Murder at the Oracle of Didyma

Murder at the Heraeum of Samos
Bias and the Adulterous Daughter
Bias and the Artists of Lebodos
Clockwork Gun- The Steampunk Adventures
of Doc Holliday

With MK Tanner
Rogue Feather
Friend or Feather

With GL Finch
Stalemate

Made in the USA
Columbia, SC
17 October 2023

24525265R00070